Mel Bay Presents

Jeff Linsky
Fingerstyle Jazz Guitar Solos

The music of Jeff Linsky with additional transcriptions and Analysis by Lenny Carlson.

cover photo by Michael Collopy

DVD Contents

1	Black Sand
2	Later
3	The Love Club
4	Up Late
5	Angel's Serenade
6	Hermosa
7	Murrieta's Farewell
8	Leo
9	Casa Miguel
10	Pacifica

Michael Spiro on percussion.

1 2 3 4 5 6 7 8 9 0

Visit us on the Web at www.melbay.com — E-mail us at email@melbay.com

Table of Contents

Introduction

When my ten-year-old fingers were first introduced to the strings of a guitar, it was a moment of incredible magic for me. It was as if the private, innermost thoughts and feelings of a sensitive, introspective kid had suddenly been given a voice. I was so taken with the instrument that I played it constantly, with only school and baths and eating and sleeping occasionally getting in the way. Too impatient for guitar lessons, it was my approach to play everything I heard by ear. Fortunately for me, I was exposed to some pretty good music early on.

There were a lot of good things that happened to me in my early years with the guitar. I attended my first Segovia concert when I was fourteen, which really opened my ears to the beautiful orchestral possibilities of the instrument. I also liked to hang out at The Lighthouse, a world-famous jazz club in Hermosa Beach, California. Although I was too young to go inside, they kept the top half of a Dutch door open to the sidewalk, so anyone could stand there and listen to all the great jazz musicians performing on stage just a few feet away. My record collection shifted from surf music and rock to classical music and jazz. I was particularly attracted to the Bossa Nova music that was just getting popular in the U.S. at the time.

When I was sixteen, I wandered into Gene Leis' Guitar Studio in Manhattan Beach. Gene was a wonderful man, very colorful and eccentric. He wasn't a virtuoso player, but he had fun with the guitar and he was an excellent businessman. Gene was supportive of everyone who wanted to play the guitar, and he sold millions of his instructional books and records worldwide. Gene apparently saw in me a very promising young guitarist; he provided me with strings (and even guitars) and allowed me to teach at his studio. It was Gene who first introduced me to Joe Pass, Vicente Gomez, Laurindo Almeida, Tommy Tedesco, Johnny de Rose, Ron Anthony and many of the other top L.A. studio guitar players.

Over the years my guitar has taken me to many parts of the globe. On my own recordings I have featured some of the best players in the world. Yet everywhere I go, it seems that there are great local players that are mostly unknown to the rest of the world. The learning never ends, and I know that everyone whose music I enjoy influences me.

This collection of music focuses on my Latin Jazz style of composing. The music is melodic and fun, and very guitar-oriented. I have sketched out polyphonic solo guitar versions of the "heads" of each tune, leaving the improvised choruses to your imagination. I want to thank Lenny Carlson for editing and assembling the music, adding tablature and providing thoughtful analysis.

I hope that the music is fun and inspiring to you.

Jeff Linsky

Foreword

Jeff Linsky is one of the finest guitarists on the contemporary jazz scene. He plays fingerstyle, on a nylon-string guitar (actually a requinto -- tuned a minor 3rd up) and renders standard tunes, original compositions and improvisations that are by turns beautiful and haunting or assertive and technically challenging. His fans include many prominent guitarists, from the best-selling artist Earl Klugh to jazz legend Jim Hall.

This book is a companion to Jeff Linsky's recent video for the Mel Bay Artist Series: **Latin Guitar Jazz Video**. There is some direct transcription, but there are also arrangements of the pieces and analysis of his style, his techniques and his approaches to certain musical problems.

The main objective of the book is to help you think as an improvisor might. Linsky plays these pieces differently every time, and he wants this free attitude to be conveyed by the contents of the book. Rather than learning every note exactly as he played it on the video, you are encouraged to study his larger musical worldview and combine what he does with your own creative music. Of course, there is a great deal to memorize on the following pages if you choose to do only that. In either case, the material presented in the book and on the video is not meant to replace other books or methods of study. An aspiring guitarist must listen, play and experience music on many levels in order to continue growing and improving.

Some awareness of Jeff Linsky's musical background is helpful. Gifted in math, he was able to visualize the fingerboard early on, and he developed a number of exercises to play simple melodies in all keys, positions and registers. He began learning standard songs by composers like Gershwin, Porter, Arlen, Jobim and others associated with the jazz tradition, and amassed an impressive repertoire of hundreds of such songs. He combined these rigorous academic aspects of musical development with the attitude that it's OK to take chances and make mistakes. *

Coming of age in Southern California, he got to know and work with Joe Pass and other important musicians. As an young adult, Jeff honed his polyphonic craft working solo guitar gigs throughout the Mediterranean, the Caribbean and Hawaii. In time, he became in-demand as an international concert artist. Along the way, he spent countless hours in the sand as a competitive beach volleyball player. This boundless energy, ambition and athletic grace are all evident in his guitar playing.

He has recorded a number of critically-acclaimed CDs for Concord and other companies and maintains an active international concert career, both as a soloist and with various ensembles. Always open to new ideas, and armed with an offbeat sense of humor, he makes joyous and very listenable music filled with surprises. Any serious student of the guitar can benefit from focusing on the art of Jeff Linsky.

Lenny Carlson

* In the section, *How to Use This Book*, there are some suggestions for developing exercises like these on your own, as well as some whys and hows of learning standard repertoire.

Jeff Linsky Discography

Passport to the Heart (1997)   Concord Vista   with Barnaby Finch, Kevin
                                    CCD-4764-2   Gibbs, Tripp Sprague, Terry
                                                     Miller, Michael Spiro, Paul
                                                     van Wageningen and Dave
                                                     Blackburn

California (1996)   Concord Vista   with Kevin Gibbs, Claudia
                                    CCD-4708   Villela, Scott Steed, Paul
                                                     van Wageningen and Michael
                                                     Spiro

Angel's Serenade (1994)   Concord Picante with Kenny Stahl, Seward
                                    CCD-4611   McCain, Michael Spiro, Karl
                                                     Perazzo and Claudia Villela

Rendezvous (1992)   Kamei   with Steve Kujala, Alphonso
                                    (KR-7006)   Johnson, Kevin Gibbs,
                                                     Michael Spiro, Karl Perazzo,
                                                     Jeff Cressman and Claudia
                                                     Villela

Solo (1992)   GSPJAZ   Solo guitar
                                    (GSP-5000)

Simpatico (1991)   GSPJAZ   with Alphonso Johnson,
                                    (GSP-7001)   Alex Acuna, Weber
                                                     Drummond, Alex Murzyn and
                                                     Jim Nichols

Up Late (1988)   Concord Picante with Steve Kujala, John
                                    CCD-4363   Leitham, Gary Cardile, Luis
                                                     Conte and Chris Trujillo

Compilations:

Jazz Celebration (1997)   Concord Jazz   with Ali Ryerson
                                    (CCD-7005)

A Concord Jazz Christmas 2   Concord   with Michael Spiro
(1996)   (CCD-4720)

The Colors of Latin Jazz: Samba! (2002)   Concord Records
                                               (CCD-5308-2)

Introduction to Latin Jazz (2000)   Concord Records   with Steve Kujala, John Leitham,
                                               (CCD-4917-2)   Luis Conte and Gary Cardile

How to Use this Book

It is assumed that the student/reader has at least several years experience as a guitarist, and knows a range of chord positions and scales. Advanced sight-reading ability is not required, but some reading facility is necessary to decipher this music on paper.

All 10 selections from Jeff Linsky's **Latin Jazz Guitar Video** are represented in this book. There is an arrangement of each piece by Jeff himself, plus some additional transcription directly from the video along with analytical text.

Choose a favorite piece with which to begin. Watch that portion of the video and listen many times to the piece. Get to the point where you really know the notes, rests, dynamics, and all the other qualities that distinguish the music. Linsky uses some standard chord forms, but often we hear melodies in counterpoint, with musical lines moving in and out and coming together in clusters. His execution on the instrument is always exemplary.

Try to isolate the separate voices that you hear in his playing. Learning to "hear" music at an advanced level is difficult; many students feel discouraged and don't put effort into such an exercise. But developing skill in this area is essential to growth as a musician.

Always take small steps in your practice. Getting one or two measures correct at a slow tempo will ensure your progress much more efficiently than trying to play a passage at performance tempo immediately. **Use a metronome to build your speed, from very slow and precise up to performance tempo.** Eventually you'll be able to play along with the video -- or other recording -- and then you can apply what you've learned to your own music.

If you are interested in developing exercises like those mentioned in the Foreword, begin with a simple melody like *Mary Had a Little Lamb*. Play the melody in the key of C -- using alternating RH fingers as in classical technique -- in open position (1st fret) on the top two strings. Then play it down an octave, using your thumb, or alternating thumb and index. Make sure that you can play it smoothly and evenly at a slow tempo before you speed up. Once you have done this, extend the exercise through the following steps:

1. Play it through the cycle of 5ths in 1st position (the cycle of 5ths is all twelve major keys set a 5th apart from each other as follows: C - G - D - A - E - B - F♯/G♭ - D♭ - A♭ - E♭ - B♭ - F). Name the notes as you play them.

2. Play it all the way up one string. The 1st string (tonic = E) requires that you begin the melody at the 4th fret (G♯), which is the major 3rd. Adjust your LH fingering first by position, playing with different fingers. Practice playing the melody using only one finger, then two. If this is done on all six strings, you will have played in the following keys: E, B, G, D, A, and E two octaves below. If you move up one fret, there will be completely different fingering, and the keys will be F, C, A♭, E♭, B♭ and F.

3. Find the same beginning notes (1st string open = 2nd string/5th fret = 3/10 = 4/14) up the neck and across the strings. Experiment with different fingerings and string combinations. Do in all 12 keys.

4. Experiment with different *pedal tones*. Hold down the tonic C in the bass while you play the melody an octave above. Then hold down the 2nd note, D. Use different fingerings. Hold down all the notes in the lower octave, and then shift, so that you are holding down a note in the higher octave while playing the melody in the bass register.

5. Play the song in other scales or modes. Changing to minor, diminished, augmented or whole tone from major changes both the sound and your fingering. Apply earlier steps to this.

6. Harmonize the melody (with supporting line below) in 2nds, major and minor 3rds, 4ths, augmented 4ths, etc., past the octave to the 13th.

7. Play the melody backwards in the bass, while playing it forward in the treble. Or play the bass in half or whole notes with the melody the melody at normal speed. Reverse bass and treble roles.

8. Play the song in two keys at once, in different registers. Your ears will never be the same. Play the melody in C major in the treble and F♯ minor in the bass, for example. There is no right and wrong in this, just different intervals producing different degrees of tension. Apply different fingerings, strings, pedal tones.

All the above can be done with a simple children's song. This is a great way to learn the fingerboard because your original frame of reference is so basic and easy to remember.

It is very important to apply your technique to the playing of *standard songs* as Jeff Linsky has. Technique doesn't exist for its own sake. Learn as many standard songs as possible. These songs, largely by American popular songwriters active during the years 1900-1960, contain common and often very attractive usages of melody, harmony and rhythm that can help guide you in the shaping of your own style and approach to performing, improvising and composing in the jazz idiom.

These songs are standard specifically because most people have heard them so much. They are part of our everyday lives. From *Over the Rainbow* to *Summertime* to *Misty* to *Satin Doll* and thousands of others, the songs are heard in supermarkets, hotels, in concerts and on recordings.

A standard is well-constructed and simple. It usually contains a *hook*, a particular musical figure or lyric that allows the song to stay with us long after hearing it. Some of the composers and lyricists who fashioned these standards had training in classical music or literature. Some were gifted jazz improvisors. Some were just "natural" talents whose efforts coincided with commercial trends of their era.

When learning a standard song, explore it thoroughly in all keys, as detailed in the *Mary Had a Little Lamb* exercise above. When attaching harmonies to the melody, start simply with triads or just a bass against the melody. A simple but well-executed arrangement is far more effective than one that is too ambitious and tense. The melody can be embellished, but with not too much ornamentation.

There are many guitarists who play beautifully in chord-melody style. Listen to recordings by George Van Eps, Joe Pass, Earl Klugh (to name a few), and of course Jeff Linsky. They all play fingerstyle and use an "orchestral" approach to the instrument. The techniques required for this approach are very advanced, but they can be mastered over time by intensive listening and practice.

Notation Practices

The transcriptions in this book are in *standard notation* and *tablature*. The tablature will help you locate the notes on the neck of the guitar. Because Jeff Linsky doesn't use tab himself, he doesn't have a preferred way to notate the music other than standard, on the *treble staff*.

Jeff has written out these particular pieces in guitar-friendly keys, but his requinto is an E♭ instrument, tuned up a minor 3rd. If you want to play in the keys he uses on the video, tune to concert pitch and then put a capo on III.

When there are several *voices* (individual parts) active, the *melody* is written with *stems up*. Because it is usually in the upper part of the staff, it is out of the way of the other voices.

The *bass* voice is written *stems down*, and is usually below the staff. The *middle voice* or voices may have stems that go either way, depending on the range of the parts at that point.

In order to avoid clutter, there are *no right hand fingerings* marked. As an improvisor, Jeff Linsky uses many different fingerings. Please see the Mel Bay Catalog for books on classical guitar technique for assistance in this area if you have questions.

There are also no *dynamics* (loud/soft) marked. The notation presents the skeleton of the music, leaving the nuances to you, the reader. Watch the video (and listen carefully) in order to develop your own approach to how to perform the music.

The following page, the beginning of *Angel's Serenade*, is a sample of the notation style to be found in the book. The terms and explanations are not used hereafter in the book.

Angel's Serenade

Jeff Linsky

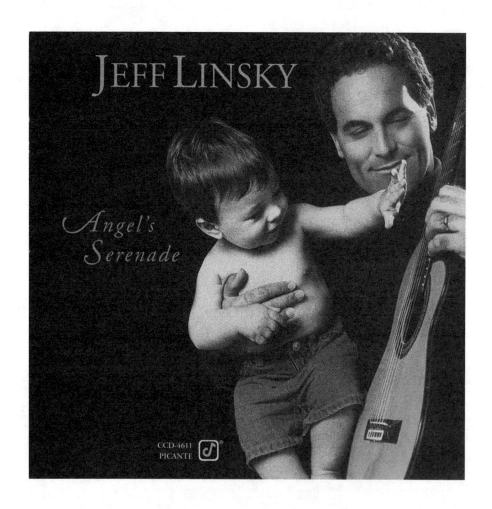

Black Sand

There are many standard songs in the jazz repertoire that fit into a short structure such as 16 measures. *Summertime*, by George and Ira Gershwin, is one; Kenny Dorham's *Blue Bossa* is another. *Black Sand* fits into this category: the meat of it, not counting the 8-bar introduction/interlude, is 16 bars long.

Black Sand is a beautiful Brazilian-influenced piece, full of lyricism and lush chords. What sets it apart is that it is played at an energetic cha cha tempo, thus combining the best of several worlds.

Jeff begins the video performance slowly with an *ad lib* improvisation. This manner of musical presentation usually includes quotes from the piece to come, giving the listener a hint of some of the melodic motives and harmonic concept. Everything is embellished -- the music flows freely without regard to strict tempo considerations and there is much *ornamentation* of the melody. Sometimes there is a *cadenza*, a particularly technical passage that leads to a V7 chord, which resolves to the I chord at the beginning of the next section.

After about 1 minute of improv, Jeff goes into tempo, aided by percussionist Michael Spiro. The 4-bar repeated intro in E minor sets up a nice syncopated rhythm. At measure 9, the chord on the downbeat is *C9♭5* (or *♯11*) which goes to *F♯m7♭5* and to the *B7♭9* (the V7) which resolves back to the tonic E minor.

Both C and F♯ (which are in a tritone relationship to each other) can resolve logically to a B dominant chord. The C moves chromatically down, and the F♯ moves up a 4th. This chromatic substitution, based on the tritone, is one of the main building blocks of modern jazz. It should be learned theoretically and practiced in all keys, with different inversions and chord formulae. There is no better way to develop harmonic facility in this style.

The melody is built on stepwise motion: F♯ to E, followed by an imitation B-A. A melodic motive (also called "germ") may be only two or three notes long. But the entire composition, if it is logically constructed, can be traced back to the initial motive. The first phrase is two measures long, and is followed by a contrasting phrase that has a different function, more rhythmic, adding no new melodic material. This kind of "tension-release" alternation of phrases is essential to the structure of the music. Adding new material, or having too much activity at this point in the exposition of the theme, destroys the natural momentum and beauty. The listener must be allowed to retain a clear memory of the melody as it unfolds.

The chord positions in this piece are not too ambitious taken individually, but the transitions must be practiced slowly so that they are smooth and seem effortless. Prior to attempting any improvising on your own, be sure you can play the melody by itself, without chords. Then add intervals or chords at the rate of one per measure, speeding up only when you are very comfortable at a slow tempo. The guitar is a harmonic instrument to be sure, but there are some limitations that do not exist on the piano. It is perhaps better to approach improvising on guitar in technical terms as if you are playing a linear (melody) instrument, augmenting your line with intervals, triads, extended chords and clusters at various points as you go along.

Black Sand

Jeff Linsky

Form: A B B A B B A B B A A

Later

Later is a good example of the difference between written and performed music. It looks like any other selection in the book, with recognizable melodies, chord forms and syncopated rhythmic figures. If played at a slow to medium tempo, it doesn't appear to be too much to handle. But Jeff Linsky has other things in mind.

He jumps out of the box with a stellar, and very up-tempo, single line introduction that is answered by percussionist Michael Spiro. All the notes are executed with precision and flair, and they remain in the listener's memory for some time into the performance. He then begins the written melody, alternating open and fretted bass notes.

Just from looking at the music, we can tell some things. Measures 2 and 6 include a repeated rhythm figure, on the & of beats 3 and 4. It's probable that when Jeff uses a device like this, the tempo of the overall piece will be fast. The chord in that measure is B♭7, and the bass notes are the root and the 5. This is a relatively static way for him to get through a measure. At a slower tempo he will often have three or four chord blocks or clusters, or melody that is ornamented with 16th and 32nd notes.

The value of a quick analysis and conclusion like this must always be judged in the context of the style of the piece and the intent of the composer or performer.

At measure 17, Jeff uses a specific type of chord voicing to establish a different feeling. Closely-voiced chords or double stops, when played as a block, have a somewhat ambiguous function, between rhythmic and harmonic. If the goal is to sound the different components clearly in a melodic sense, they need to be spread out a little more, with wider intervals between the voices. Major or minor 2nd intervals have a very characteristic sound. In this case, the *D min 6* uses the open B string, which has its own resonance and timbre. This chord, when allowed to ring for a bit longer, is a very romantic and guitaristic sound.

The written music is a guide, and it gives us insight into the compositional processes that someone like Jeff Linsky goes through en route to realizing a musical piece. To play in his style, one must do more than interpret, however. One can expand a great deal upon the written music with the help of the video and, of course, with your own imagination and effort.

Later

Jeff Linsky

fine

2x then D.C.

The Love Club

After an ad lib introduction on the video (improvised as is his custom), Jeff Linsky sets a medium tempo. *The Love Club* has a number of symmetrical phrases that are connected by the syncopated rhythm stated in measure 1.

The difference between the first four measures at A and the first ending demonstrates in textbook fashion one of the basic rules of musical form: the antecedent and consequent phrase structure. The *F#minor* (relative minor to A, tonic key of the piece) moves to a *G9*, which functions as a substitute for the dominant *C#7*, repeats and then resolves to the mediant *C#m7*. Note the ascending bass movement in mm. 14-15.

The 1st ending has a sequential melody that begins on the 3rd degree. The harmony begins this time on the tritone (*D#m7*) and has a descending bass line. The sequence (which is a general imitation of the previous four measures) also has -- in the written version -- a greater thickness of texture in the 3rd measure (21) and a more active last measure (22).

To learn to construct music that observes such rules of form and symmetry is a worthy goal. What Jeff does with ease on an improvisational basis is the result of many years of intensive application: critical listening, practice and analysis. Study *The Love Club* with these ideas in mind.

The Love Club

Jeff Linsky

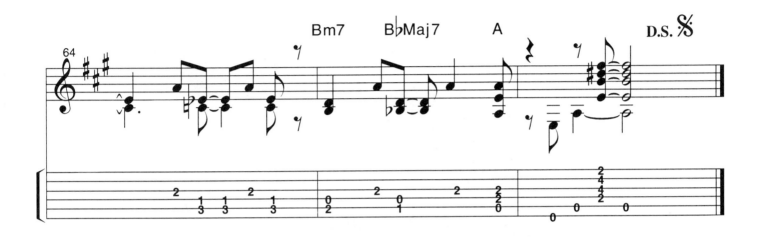

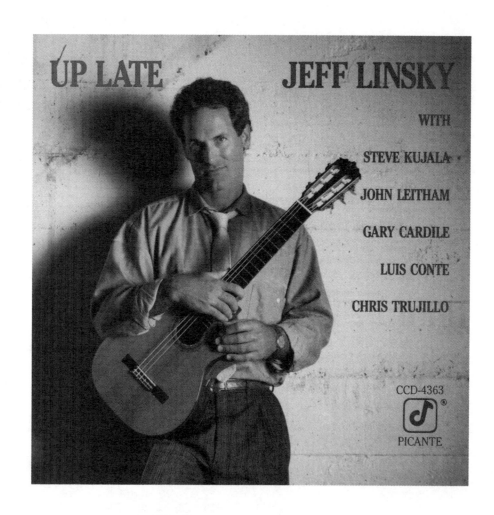

Up Late

Watch out! One slip of the finger and this runaway train will be over the mountains and through the woods. Not only is the tempo on *Up Late* very quick, but the melodic syncopation (3/3/2) of the Introduction complicates matters further by forcing three chord changes in rapid succession off-the-beat.

Don't let melodrama take over here. With enough application, most readers will be able to play this piece. The trick (not a real trick) is to play everything slowly in rhythm -- and very precisely -- until you can move it up to performance tempo.

There is no need to hurry through this kind of drill. Jeff Linsky's pieces, like most well-constructed music, have value when performed at any tempo, because they are transparent and quite rich in melodic, rhythmic and harmonic material and development. Everything that you are doing now (and always, for that matter) with your music is a process. Once you learn *Up Late* or another flagwaver to your satisfaction, you'll go on to something else. It's all cumulative; any effort is always rewarded.

Besides the tempo and the syncopation concerns, the structure of the written piece is relatively simple. The first four-measure (at **A**) begins in D dorian and ends with a transition to F Major. The second phrase (m. 13) provides marked contrast, melodically, harmonically and rhythmically.

Section **B** is completely different: a much calmer feeling, a true release from the intense activity of the earlier section. The shape of the melody is relatively static through mm. 27-29, with m. 30 having a different rhythm and a dominant harmony to prepare for a repeat of the theme. The Coda is a repeat of the 3/3/2 pattern from the intro alternating with percussion fills. (For solo guitar playing, Jeff has added some optional guitar fills.)

The more you analyze this music, even in the simple terms we've used here, the more understanding you'll gain about what makes music work. Even if the listener is not aware of the motives, modulations, rhythmic interplay of the voices and all the other structural devices, the fact that the music is well-constructed makes all the difference. Once you see what is happening theoretically with the music in this book and other music that you study, your own work will assume a new sense of structure and purpose. That's progress!

Up Late

Jeff Linsky

Angel's Serenade

This selection departs a bit from the improvisatory focus of the video -- and Jeff's playing in general -- but the results are very satisfying. *Angel's Serenade* is a masterpiece of concept and composition for guitar and, as always, Jeff's execution is flawless.

Angel's Serenade is a set piece, and should be practiced as written. It is remarkably lyrical music, reminiscent of the great Spanish Romantic composers of the 19th century, and sounds like something Segovia himself might have played. That Jeff Linsky writes music of this calibre speaks volumes about his stature in the world of guitarists.

On the video, Jeff repeats the music from beginning to end. There are no chord positions or voicings indicated on the music, but the tab, string and fingering indications should give you all the help you need to practice it. The Roman numerals refer to barre positions (i.e. IV = barre at fourth fret).

Jeff plays the piece as a solo on the video. It is recommended that you compare this performance with his Concord Picante CD, *Angel's Serenade* (CCD-4611), on which the guitar melody is subordinated to Claudia Villela's vocal. Both are inspired treatments, and there may be something in each that will inspire you.

As you work with this book and the video, there will be many opportunities to pull out all stops and show just how fast and tricky you can play. *Angel's Serenade*, with its unique and stirring qualities, is not one of them. A slow, legato and very expressive execution is the most effective. Your own musicianship will be greatly enhanced by the experience of bringing such a beautiful work to life.

Angel's Serenade

Jeff Linsky

36

Play 2x

Hermosa

Hermosa begins with a figure reminiscent of Jobim's *One-Note Samba*, at a bright tempo that incorporates a repetitive eighth-note melody with syncopated chords. The harmonies are standard chromatic variants of the ii - V - I (or iii) - vi progression that makes up so much of the literature of jazz.

Note the ascending movement in measure 4: *F♯ min - G7 - G♯m*. The *G7* is a chromatic substitute for *B7*. How might this work? Play the following resolutions: *G7-CMaj7, B7-CMaj7, G7-F♯Maj7, G7-EMaj7, F7-EMaj7, B7-B♭Maj7, B7-EMaj7, B7-G♯min7, G7-G♯min7, G7- G♯Maj7, G7-Cmin, B7-Cmin , B7-Emin , B7-F♯min, B7-F♯Maj7*. Think of others that might fit into this group. Listen and compare. Which progressions are the "strongest," that is, most suggestive of a coventional V-I relationship. Which ones are more mysterious or remote? Try the chords in inversions, not just with the root in the bass. All of the above combinations are used in jazz.

The basic progression outlined at A is I - IV7 - iii - ii. The dominant function, resolving back to the I, is handled by the pick-up notes *b-c♯-e*. This is not as strong a progression as is I -IV- V, but there is much more subtlety and jazz flavor. Going from the IMaj7 to the IV7 is a well-used device in standard songs (*On a Clear Day, I'm Confessin' That I Love You, Broadway*, many others), but it is a great sound, bluesy and full of movement.

The ornamentation at measure 9 heightens the sense of movement. In most types of music, figures such as this one in 32nd notes are not part of the core melody, because such a figure moves too fast to be understood by the listener. Often 8ths and quarters convey the melody. The listener's memory retains these larger subdivisions much more easily.

The last beat of measure 9 is a dominant type chord built on the II, which affects a transition to the key of B Major (the V of the original key). The I -IV7 is imitated in this new tonality. Compare the G7 in m. 9 with the one in m. 11. How do the functions differ? How effective is the choice of chords in keeping the movement going at this point?

At B, the bass is in half notes (notwithstanding the eighth rests). This allows the player and listener to concentrate on the melodic movement in the upper voices. If there is an overactive and lengthy unison rhythm feeling between the voices, the tension becomes too great. For example, if a syncopated 16th figure like dah - dah - dah - DOT, dah - dah - dah - DOT is played once or twice or as an interlude using full chords, it can be very exciting. If it becomes the basis of the piece, its effectiveness is lessened.

Many jazz musicians don't articulate these theoretical concepts using such academic terms. They simply integrate the concepts over decades of listening and playing in the tradition. Some, like Jeff Linsky, teach themselves, and evolve their own method of how to function in the world of music theory. There are numerous paths to the top of the mountain.

Hermosa

Jeff Linsky

Form: A B C D E C D A B E

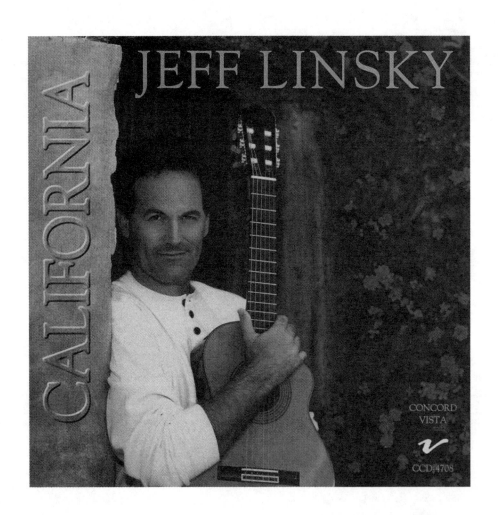

Murrieta's Farewell

Dedicated to the famous Mexican bandit and folk-hero Joaquin Murrieta, this selection represents a slight change from the general direction of the music in this book. Like *Angel's Serenade*, it has an old world quality. There are, however, significant differences between those two pieces, and there are more ornamental and other characteristics "beyond the page" than you will find with some of the other music. The written part should be approached as a guide, with chord symbols and fingerings along with the melody helping you to realize your own version of this charming and evocative work.

There is a very idiomatic Spanish flavor to the ad lib intro that Jeff develops on the video. The main characteristics of this style are florid embellishment, tremolo, and the harmonic resolution ♭VI-V (Phrygian cadence). In this case the chords are *C* to *B* or *B7*. Flamenco guitar music -- the national folk/gypsy music of Spain, with input from Africa and the Middle East -- is marked by such characteristics. Jeff adds to this some Mexican-sounding 3rds and 6ths, very romantic with extensive vibrato.

The tempo is slow but rhythmic. Unlike many of the other pieces, there is not a sense of chord melody style a la Joe Pass or George Van Eps, but rather a thinner, more transparent texture. The melody appears first, followed by a full chord, bass line or fill that answer to the melody.

The first chord after the introduction is *B minor*, which is the mediant chord (III) of the relative major G. This chord fits into the *E natural minor* scale which derives from the 6th degree of the G scale. The natural minor scale is an exact transposition, with no additional accidentals (sharps or flats). The mediant chord has its own characteristic sound, almost a tonic -- chord of resolve -- but not quite. Although built on the fifth degree of E minor, it has none of the "pull" of a true dominant chord such as *B* or *B7*. A true dominant chord always includes a leading tone to the tonic,which in this case is E. The leading tone, which is the major 3rd of the dominant, rises 1/2 step to resolve to resolve to the root of the tonic or I chord.

In traditional *diatonic* harmony, chords built on the I, III and VI of a major scale are stable, that is, they contain a sense of resolution (*chromatic* harmony is a different matter). Chords built on the II, IV, V and VII are *tension* chords which must move elsewhere to resolve. Both tension and resolution chords are rather fluid in jazz, and different triads or partials freely substitute for one another. Any chords with two common tones can do this.

What is the point of all this theory? Well, if you have a goal of composing or playing jazz or classical music that has the depth, complexity and beauty of Jeff Linsky's work, you need to know something about music theory. You can do it all by ear, as Django Reinhardt, Wes Montgomery and prescious few others in history have done, or you can make it a bit easier on yourself and learn what are actually a few simple mathematical formulae to give your own creative efforts some structure. However you do it, the theory (which functions like grammar does in written and spoken language) must be thoroughly integrated into the overall musical effort. The end product, the music itself, is a result of theory, technique and inspiration, a combination that requires a lifetime commitment, at the very least.

Murrieta's Farewell

Jeff Linsky

FORM: B C A B C A ⊕

Leo

Written for Jeff's son, this piece has a slightly mysterious quality, perhaps reflective of the mysteries of childhood (and parenthood). There are shifts in tonality throughout along with deceptive -- and rather remote -- harmonic movement.

The out-of-tempo introduction of 8 bars gives us the "germ" of *Leo*, a 3-note arpeggio followed by a half-step descent to the tritone. Look for this figure, either literal or imitated, to recur often. On a compositional level, the use of a tritone takes the listener away from the initial feeling of key. The first two measures are in G, followed by a shift to a 3rd-related tonality. At measure 6, the tritone reappears, this time in the form of a shift from *B♭* to *E* (minor). Because there is a sense of closure at measure 8 (essentially a *Emin6*), and because the coda is in E, one can say that E is the key of the piece.

The contrasting section at measure 20 is in F. Note the different rhythmic figures and other devices he uses for variety.

Leo

Jeff Linsky

Form: A B A B A

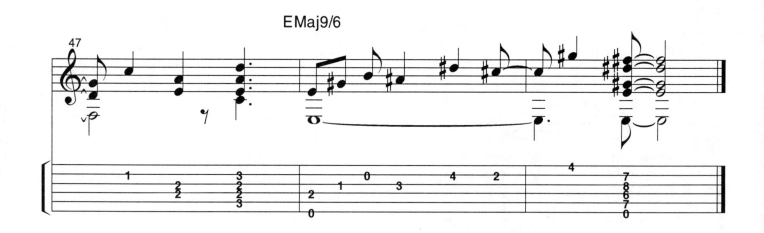

Casa Miguel

This piece is a feature for Michael Spiro, hence the name. On the video, Michael holds forth with all manner of sounds, including different tambourines, whistles, shakers, bongos and conga. Because of the elevation of the percussion to nearly co-equal status with Jeff Linsky's guitar, the music itself changes.

If a lead instrument is to share "top billing" in this fashion, some changes *must* occur in the music. These changes can be expressed through a lessening of the volume (or other dynamic aspects), harmonies that are thinner or don't have characteristics that attract attention, or simplicity of melody and harmony. If such a change is not written into the music and undertaken willingly by the lead instrumentalist, the effect will be lost, and it will appear that there are two forces fighting for the limelight. Such ego battles never serve the larger musical purpose. Unfortunately, they exist nonetheless, often due to insecurity or insensitivity on the part of some musicians.

Jeff and Michael engage in a lively dialogue that allows each to shine. The difference between this and some of the other pieces in the collection is that there are long interludes between the complex melody sections, where Jeff rhythmically vamps between two chords, while Michael takes center stage.

Why is this important? If you want to compose your own music or arrange the music of other people for different instruments, you must consider such elements as timbre, dynamics and thickness of texture. There is no way to successfully manipulate all of these elements without thinking as a "team player."

Casa Miguel

Jeff Linsky

Pacifica

Pacifica is a medium bossa, prefaced on the video by a brief out-of-tempo introduction. It is an excellent example of motivic development. A *motive* (or germ) can be melodic, rhythmic or harmonic. It is the core of any composition, and is usually not longer than a measure in length.

The syncopated rhythm figure in measure 1 is the main motive of the piece, recurring in many forms throughout. Note the expansion of the motive in m. 2, with the *e* note of the melody dropping 1/2 step and the *b* going up to *d* (a minor 3rd). Combining the "jazzy" quality of a secondary dominant harmony (F13) with this expansion takes the sequence beyond the level of pure imitation. Subsequent harmonic and melodic movement sustains the interest level of the listener.

There has to be enough movement and variety in the exposition and development of motives in this style of music to justify the intense creative effort. Music that is simpler in structure, such as rock, blues, country or pop and folk styles, can be satisfying because we are *listening for different things*. Jeff Linsky's music contains movement on many levels, and we expect certain things as listeners. For example, he may have several chord changes in a measure, or a lot of melodic ornamentation. This is normal for his style and level of performance skill. For Jeff to play one simple chord or melodic figure over many measures would not be appropriate. Conversely, to hear someone like Johnny Cash or John Lee Hooker play through chord changes and complex rhythmic and melodic passages, as Jeff does, would fundamentally alter their music and how we perceive it.

At letter **B**, there are two voices with apparently conflicting notation -- the note F♯ in the bass figure interrupts the sustained 6th interval. Don't worry about interpreting this literally; it can't be done. Understand the *intent*, which is to sustain the upper voice and give it a singing quality. As another example of intent, occasionally a composer, even one with extensive training in instrumentation, will write notes or a passage out of the range of a particular instrument. There may be a certain style or concept he/she is attempting to communicate to the performer.

Above all of the theoretical discussion, the most important thing is to enjoy this joyous and well-executed music, and to experience the wonders of beautiful and subtle harmonic and melodic movement.

   Note: Intro is played on the video. It is not notated in the music.

Pacifica

Jeff Linsky

Form: Intro B B1 C B B1 C B1 C A B1 C B ⊕

D.S. al Coda

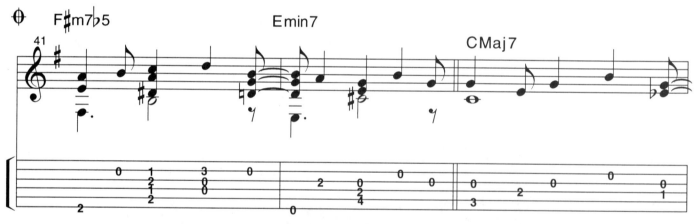

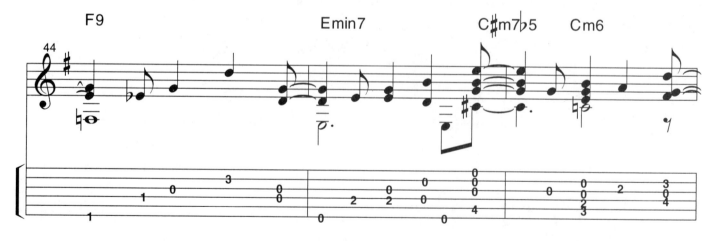

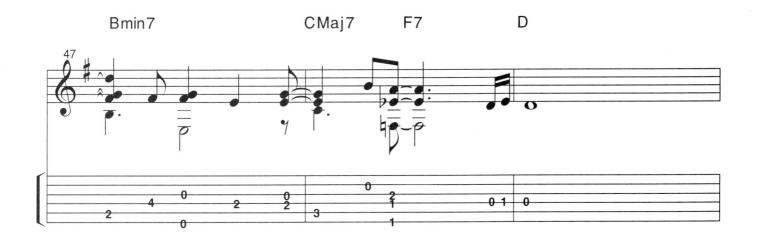

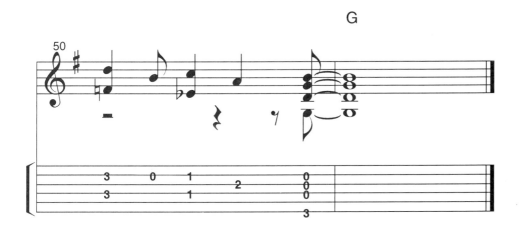

Conclusion

The guitar is a marvelous instrument, complex and mysterious, capable of yielding great pleasure and/or frustration. Jeff Linsky has reached the highest level as a composer, performer and improvisor on the guitar, and it is very worthwhile to spend time with his music and performance video.

The psychology of this learning situation is critical. To be creative, to integrate new information, to refine the technical aspects of a particular form of artistic expression (in other words, to make satisfying music), one must be open, without ego conflict, and capable of surrendering to the process. It is, after all, a lifetime process, and an artist may learn something new every day, both in the art itself and from the world around us.

If you have worked with Jeff Linsky's material, not only will your own musical skills have advanced significantly, but your artistic worldview will be more mature and you will be closer to making music that is truly expressive of your own personality. There is no better way for an aspiring guitarist to learn.

It has been a pleasure working with Jeff on this book, and I hope that you, the reader, have gained as much from the experience as I have.

LC

Lenny Carlson

Lenny Carlson has authored numerous books of guitar transcriptions and analysis for Mel Bay and other publishing companies. His most recent books are *Jack Jezzro: Acoustic Dreams* (Mel Bay, 1998) and *John Jackson: Don't Let Your Deal Go Down* (Arhoolie/Mel Bay, 1998) Artists included in his list of titles include blues pioneers John Lee Hooker, Lonnie Johnson and Willie Dixon, rocker Neil Young, Bahamian folk guitarist Joseph Spence and classical guitarist Stevan Pasero. He has written articles for *Acoustic Guitar* and *Fingerstyle Guitar* magazines.

An accomplished jazz guitarist, Lenny is also an award-winning composer and arranger who has produced two albums of his original music. A selection from the second album, *In the Mud*, was nominated for a Grammy as Best Jazz Instrumental Composition. One of his arrangements is featured on *Noel Noel*, a Christmas, 1996 CD by the Camilli String Quartet on the Sugo label. He designed music and sound effects for video games in the early 1980s and has since composed for videos and films. He is currently arranging and performing as accompanist for jazz/pop vocalist Millicent Wood and doing free-lance music writing assignments in the San Francisco Bay area.

Lenny Carlson received a Master's Degree in Music Performance from Portland State University in Oregon. He is on the Music Faculties at City College of San Francisco and the Music/Recording Industry Program at San Francisco State University. A native of Los Angeles, he now lives in San Francisco with his wife and two daughters.

Jeff Linsky

With a strong classical guitar technique and a remarkable gift for improvisation, Jeff Linsky has developed his own warmly passionate and personal style of playing, blending elements of jazz, classical, and Latin music.

"This astonishing guitarist seems to have bridged entirely
the troublesome gap between brain and fingers."
~ Acoustic Guitar Magazine

A native of Southern California, Jeff discovered the guitar at the age of ten. Although primarily a self-taught musician, he did study briefly with both Spanish guitar virtuoso Vicente Gomez and jazz great Joe Pass. While still in his teens, Jeff began to travel the world as a guitarist. Always interested in experiencing different cultures and musical influences, he met and performed in concert with an international variety of world-renowned artists, from American jazz legend Jim Hall to the respected Brazilian maestro Carlos Barbosa-Lima.

"Jeff is one of my favorite players. He has it all – great technique,
a fabulous sound, and a wonderful feel for the instrument!"
~ Earl Klugh

Jeff "paid his dues" as a performer in such remote outposts as Hawaii, the Caribbean and the Mediterranean, never once complaining about having to endure another summer in the South of France. In 1988, he signed with Concord Records, releasing the very successful CD "Up Late" that year.

"If, for some unfathomable reason, Latin Jazz has not yet gotten
into your blood or touched your soul, then this is the album
(Up Late) that will make you a believer!"
~ Jazzscene Magazine

Jeff continued to compose in a Latin Jazz style on his next project, "Simpatico" (GSPJAZ), featuring Weather Report veterans Alphonso Johnson and Alex Acuna. Although Jeff's next five CD's varied in style, from the more jazzy, improvised "Solo" (GSPJAZ) to the contemporary jazz-pop project, "Passport to the Heart" (Concord), Jeff is still perhaps best known as a Latin Jazz artist. He has even been named an "Honorary Hispanic" by *Latin Beat Magazine*. The Mel Bay Artist Series video, "Jeff Linsky, Latin Guitar Jazz", further reinforces that perception.

"Jeff's ability to create memorable melodies and
dazzling improvisation is a joy to experience."
~ Just Jazz Guitar

Beyond his recording and international concert career, Jeff also composes for film and television. His music can be heard around the world.

Jeff Linsky's website: http://jefflinsky.com